T0193292

المختصرات البحرية الدولية

اعداد: الربان البحري

محمد جواد علي القرغولي

مراجعة واشراف

ديانا زويد : الاستاذة

ماجستير الادب الانكليزي

المختصرات البحرية الدولية
اعداد: الربان البحري

محمد جواد علي القرغولي

ربان اعالي البحار

الطبعة العربية الأولى 2012م

رقم الإيداع لدى دائرة المكتبة الوطنية 938/ 3 /2012

ISBN 978 – 9957 – 551- 43 - 8

دار الجنان للنشر والتوزيع

المركز الرئيسي(التوزيع - المكتبة) المملكة الأردنية الهاشمية

تلفاكس 0096264659891 ص. ب 927486 الرمز البريدي11190

مكتب السودان ـ الخرطوم 00249918064984

E-mail:dar_jenan@yahoo.com

اعداد الربان البحري

محمد جواد علي القرغولي

ربان اعالي البحار

مراجعة واشراف

الاستاذة : ديانا زويد

ماجستير الادب الانكليزي

تقديم

يقول الدكتور جنسن،آن كل من يؤلف كتابا فانه يطمح إلى المديح،أما مـن

يعد قاموسا فحسبه أن ينجوا من اللوم.

لا شك أني بذلت أقصى جهدي في سبيل وضع جميع المختصرات البحرية

بعد ان أمضيت أكثر من عامين وأنا اقرأ وأراجـع جميـع الكتـب البحريـة

الصادرة ومن غير استثناء في سبيل إعداد هذا الكتاب الذي أقدمـه هديـة

متواضعة لكل زملائي البحريين العاملين على ظهـر البحـر وفي جميـع أنـواع

السفن وأرجو أن يحقق الكتاب غاياته والفائدة المنشودة في رفد المكتبـة

البحرية العربية بمثل هـذه الكتـب لفائـدة الجميع،فالكتـاب لـيس للبـارة

فحسب،إنما للعاملين في قطاع النقل البحري والشركات التجارية والموانئ.

5

حيث أننا بـشر ،فالإنـسان ليـس معصوما مـن الخطاء،ولذلك فاني أقدم

اعتذاري مسبقا عن أي خلل قد يلمسه القارئ الكريم ليمنحني العـذر في

ذلـك،كما وان العلـوم والتكنولوجيـا في قطـاع النقـل البحري في تقدم

متواصل،لذلك فان العديد من المختصـرات الحديثة قد تكـون ظهـرت،أو

التي سـتظهر حـديثا ولم يحتويهـا الكتـاب،عن ذلك أقدم اعتـذاري أيضا

وأتمنى من كل قلبي ان يكون الكتاب عونا مفيدا لكل الدارسين والباحثين

عن المختصرات وان يرفدني زمـلائي بكـل ملاحظـاتهم النقديـة بخصوص

الكتاب.

وفي الختام أتمنى للجميـع خـالص تحيـاتي ومـن الله التوفيق وبـه نـستعين

والحمد لله رب العالمين .

الربان محمد جواد علي القرغولي /2012

<u>A</u>

A	Ampere; Amplitude: Away Arctic:Antarctic:Altitude
AA	Antiaircraft
AA	Certificate issued to a ship indicating crew matters are in order
AAA	American Automobile Association
AAAAA	American Association against Acronym Abuse
AAAS	American Association for the Advancement of Science
AACS	Automatic Access Control System (computer)
AAEW	Atlantic Airborne Early Warning
AAPA	American Association for Port Authorities

AAR	Against All Risks
AARP	American Association for Retired Persons
AAS	Associate in Applied Science
AASCU	American Association of State Colleges and Universities
AAU	Amateur Athletic Union
AAUP	American Association of University Professors
AAUW	American Association of University Women
ABAND	Abandoned
AB	Able Bodied (seaman)
ABA	American Bankers Association
ABA	American Booksellers Association
ABCC	Association of British Chambers of Commerce

ABI	Automatic Broker Interface
ABI	Automatic Broker Interface (freight forwarding)
ABLJ	Adjustable Buoyancy Life Jacket
ABP	Associated British Ports
ABS	Air Breathing System
ABS	American Bureau of Shipping
ABS	Anchor Bolt Stabilizer
ABS	Artificial Buoyant Seabed
ABS	Antilock Braking System
ABS	Auto Backup System
ABS	Automatic backup Shutdown
ABS	Automated Balancing System
A.C	Athletic Club
AC	Air conditioning

AC	Alternating Current; Altocumulus
AC	Before Christ (ante christum)
AC	Area Code
ACAS	Advisory, Conciliation & Arbitration Service
ACC	Area Control Centre
ACC	Antarctic Circumpolar Current
ACD	Automatic Call Distribution
ACE	American Council on Education
ACL	Approved Carriage List
ACL	Atlantic Container Line
ACLU	American Civil Libraries Union
ACMP	Advisory Committee on Marine Pollution
ACO	Air Craft Coordinator
ACOP	Approved Code of Practice

ACP	African, Caribbean and Pacific
ACS	American Chemical Society
ACT	Aqaba Container Terminal
ACV	Actual Cash Value
ACV	Air-Cushion Vehicle
AD	Accidental Damage (insurance)
AD	Anno Domini
AD	Active Duty
AD	Assistant Director
AD	Air Dried
ADA	Average Daily Attendance
ADB	Accidental Death Benefit
ADC	Air Defense Command
ADC	Analog-to-Digital Converter
ADC	Aide to Dependent Children

ADD	Attention Deficit Disorder
ADF	Automatic Direction Finder
ADF	Automatic Document Feeder (communication)
ADIZ	Air Defense Identification Zone
AND	European Inland Waterway Recommendations for DG
ADOS	Additional Observations (meteorology)
ADP	Automatic Data Processing
ADPC	Abu Dhabi Port Company
ADR	Accident Data Recorder
ADR	European Agreement Concerning Int. Carriage of DG By Road
ADT	Average Daily Traffic
ADX	Automatic Digital Exchange
AE	Third Class Ship in Lloyd's Register (insurance)

AEB	Acquisition Exclusion Boundary
AEC	Atomic Energy Commission
AEE	Automatic Evaluation Equipment
AERO	Aeronautical
AEI	Automatic Equipment Identification
AES	Aeronautical Earth Station
AEVR	Approved for the carriage of Explosives in a Vehicle
AEW	Airborne Early Warning
AF	Air Force/ Associated Fisheries
AF	Audio Frequency
AFB	Air Force Base
AFC	Automatic Frequency Control
AFD	Accelerated Freeze Dried
AFL	American Federation of Labor

AFN	Aeronautical Fix Network
AFR	Accident Frequency Rate
AFTN	Aeronautical Fixed Telecommunication Network
AFTRA	American Federation of Television and Radio Artists
AG	Anti Grounding
AG	Attorney General
AGC	Advanced Graduate Certificate
AGC	Automatic Gain Control
AGP	Azimuth Gain Plot
AGT	Advanced Gas Turbine
AGV	Automatic Guided Vehicle
AHA	American Heart Association
AHTS	Anchor Handling Tug Supply
AHTS	Anchor Handling Towing Supply Vessel

AHTS	Anchor Handling Tug Support (vessel)
AIMU	American Institute of Marine Underwriters
AHTS	Anchor Handling Tug Supply
AHV	Anchor Handling Vessel
AI	Air interception
AI	Artificial Intelligence
AIA	American Institute of Architect
AID	Agency for International Development
AID	Artificial Insemination by Donors
AIDS	Acquired Immunodeficiency syndrome
AIEE	American Institute of Electrical Engineers
AIME	Associate of the Institute of Marine Engineers
AIMU	American Institute of Marine Underwriters

AIP	Aeronautical Information Publication
AIRMET	Weather forecast for the civil aviation
AIS	Aeronautical Information Service
AIS	Accident Investigation Site
AIS	Acoustic Intercept System
AIS	Air Injection System
AIS	Alarm Indication Signal
AIS	Antenna Interface System
AIS	Annual Inspection Survey
AIS	Auto Insurance Specialist
AIS	Automated Intercept System
AIS	Automatic Information System
AISM	Association International de Signalization Maritime
AIT	Auto Ignition Test

AKA	Also Known As
AKD	Auto Kick Down
ALA	American Library Association
ALI	Automatic Location Identification
ALRS	Admiralty List of Radio Signals
AM	Amplitude Modulation
AM	Ante Meridian (before Noon)
AMD	Advanced Multi- Hull Design
AMES	Association of Marine Engineers School
AMIRIS	Advanced Maritime Infrared Imaging System
AMMI	American Merchant Marine Institute
AMR	Automatic Message Routing
AMS	Aeronautical Mobile Service
AMSA	Australian Maritime Safety Authority

AMSL	Above Marine Sea Level
AMSLAN	American Sign Language
AMS(R)	Aeronautical Mobile Satellite (route) Service
AMSS	Aeronautical Mobile Satellite Service
AMT	Advanced Marine Technology
AMT	Association of Marine Traders
AMU	Atomic Mass Unit
AMVERS	Automated Mutual-Assistance Vessel Rescue/Report System
ANC	African National Congress
ANF	Arrival Notification Form
ANI	Atomic Number Identification
ANMS	Automated Notice to Mariners System
ANOVA	Analysis of Variance
ANPR	Automatic Number Plate Recognition

ANSI	American National Standards Institute
ANTS	Automatic Navigation & Track Keeping System
AOB	Any Other Business
AOL	Auto Oil programmed
AORE	Atlantic Ocean Region East Satellite
AORW	Atlantic Ocean Region West Satellite
AP	Additional Premium
AP	Associated Press
AP	Assumed Position
APCRS	Amplifier Piston Common-Rail System
APEX	Advanced-Purchased Excursion (passenger transport)
API	Air Pollution Indicator/Index
API	American Petroleum Institute
APL	Adjustable Pressure Limiting

APL	Automatic Premium Loan
APL	Automatic Programming Language
APO	Army Post Office
APOTA	Automatic Positioning Telemetering Antenna
APP	Aft Perpendicular
APR	Annual Percentage Range
APT	After Peak Tank
APT	Automatically Programmed Tool
AQ	Accomplishment Quotient
AR	Acknowledgement/Advice of Receipt
AR	Account Receivable
AR	All Risks Return
ARC	Accelerated Response Centre
ARC	AIDS - related complex

ARC	American Red Cross
ARCS	Admiralty Raster Chart System/Service
ARM	Adjustable rate mortgage
ARPA	Automatic Rader Plotting Aid
A.R	Acknowledgement of receipt
AR	All Risks
ARP	Air raid precautions
ARPA	Automatic Radar Plotting Aid
ARTM	Approved Requirements& Testing Methods(DG)
AS	After sight/All Sections
AS	Air speed
AS	Anti-submarine
ASA	American Standards Association
ASAP	As soon as possible

ASCE	American Society of Civil Engineers
ASDAR	Aircraft to Satellite Data Relay
ASE	American Stock Exchange
ASE	An Association of Southeast Asian Nation
ASF	Additional Secondary Phase Factor
ASF	Associate of the Institute of Shipping & Forwarding agent
ASLI	Automatic Safe Load Indicator
ASME	American Society of Merchant Engineers
ASN	Average Sample Number
ASN	Advanced Shipping Note
ASOS	Automatic Storm Observation Service
ASQC	American Society of Quality Control
ASR	Air-to-Sea Rescue
ASR	Automatic Storage & Retrieval Systems

A/SRS	AIR Sea Rescue Service
ASRT	Academy of Scientific Research and Technology
AST	Above Ground Storage Tank
ASTM	American Society for Testing Materials
ASW	Anti-Submarine Warfare
AT	Accompanied Trailer (Ro-Ro)
AT	Air Temperature/Accompanied Trailer
AT	Automatic Time/Atlantic Time
ATA	American Transport Association
ATAC	Automated Tracking & Control
ATC	Automatic Temperature Control
ATCC	Air Traffic Control center (aviation)
ATD	Actual Time of Departure
ATE	Automatic Test Equipment

ATIS	Advanced Transport Information System
ATIS	Automated Terminal Information Services
ATLAS	Automatic Tabulating, Listing and Sorting
ATM	Active Transport Management
ATM	Automatic Teller Machine (banking)
ATM	Automatic Tracking & Monitoring Device
ATOL	Appropriate Technology for Developing Countries
ATR	Approved Tank Requirements (DG)
ATRAN	Automatic Terrain Recognition & Navigation
ATS	Anchored Towing Supply Vessel
ATS	Air Traffic System
ATSDR	Agency for Toxic materials and Disease Registry
AU	Astronomical Unit

AUSREP	Australian Ships Reporting System
AV	Audio Visual
AVR's	Approved Vehicle Requirements (DG)
AWACS	Airborne Warning & Control System
AWS	All Water

<u>B</u>

B	Bar
BA	Breathing Apparatus
BA	Bill of Health
BA	British Admiralty
BACAT	Barge –Aboard –Catamaran
BAL	Blood- Alcohol Level
BAF	Bunker Adjustable Factor
BAMA	British Amesterdam Maritime Association

BAPS	Beacon Automated Processing System
BATNEEC	Best Available Technology Not Entailing Excessive Cost
BB	Blue Book
BBB	Before Breaking Bulk
BBE	Best Before End Date
BDI	Both Days Included
BCF	Bio Concentration Factor
BCO	Biochemical Oxygen Demand
BFI	Baltic Freight Index
BFWA	Broadband Fixed Wireless Access
BGV	Bateau Grande Vitess
BI	British Imperial System
BICERI	British Internal Combustion Engine Research Institute

BIFA	British International Freight Association
BIFFEX	Baltic International Freight Futures Exchange
BITE	Built-In Test Equipment
BMS	Bachelor of Marine Science
BE	Bill of Entry
BE	Bill of exchange
BD	Bank Draft
BDI	Both Days Included
BFI	Baltic Freight Index
BFO	Beat Frequency Oscillator
BIH	Bureau Internationale de L'Heure
BIMCO	Baltic & International Maritime Conference
BIPM	International Bureau of Weights & measures

B/L	Bill of Lading/Bulk Load
BLEVE	Boiling Liquid Expanding Vapor Explosion
BLO	Below Clouds (meteorology)
BLSN	Blowing Snow (meteorology)
BMI	Body Mass Index
BNS	Bathymetric Navigation System
BOCE	Board of Customs and Excise
BOD	Biochemical Oxygen Demand
BOE	Barrel of Oil Equivalent
BOO	Build-On-Operate
BOT	Build-Operate Transfer
BOTB	British Overseas Trade Board
PIA	British Ports Industry Association
BPIA	British Ports Industry Association

BS	British Standards
BSC	British Shippers 'Council
BSFL	British Shipping Federation Limited
BSH	British Sailors'' Institute
BSI	British standards Institution
BSRA	British Ship Research Association
BTAC	Brewery Transport Advisory Committee
BTU	British Thermal Unit
BUSHIPS	Bureau of Ships
BV	Bureau VERITAS (classification)
BVL	Bundesvereinigung Logistik (German)
BWB	British Waterways Board
BWM	Ballast Water Management
BWMC	Ballast Water Management Cleaning

<u>C</u>

C	Celsius: Compass: Correction: Course
CA	Collision Avoidance
CABAF	Currency & Bunker Adjustment Factor
CAC	Central Arbitration Committee
CAD	Cisco Agent desktop
CAD	Cash against Documents/Delivery
CAD	Confined Aquatic Disposal
CAF	Cost and Freight Insurance
CALM	Catenary Anchor Leg Mooring
CAN	Customs Assigned Number
CAP	Central Alerting Post
CAT	Computer Assist Translation
CB	Container Base/Currency Bond

CBD	Cash before Delivery
CBT	Computer Based Training
CFD	Computational Fluid Dynamic
CAD	Computer Aided Detection
CB	Compass Bearing
CBDR	Constant Bearing, Decreasing Range
CBT	Clean Ballast Tank
CC	Compass Course
CC	Chamber of Commerce
CC	Chronometer correction
CCC	Custom Clearance Certificate
CCIR	International Radio Consultative Committee
CCIT	International Telecommunication Consultative Committee
CCR	Capacity Constrained Resource

CCR	Chief Officer Control Room
CCRS	Community Cargo Release System
CCT	Common Custom Tariff
CCTV	Close Circuit Television
CCU	Consultative Committee for Units ofWeights and Measurements
CCW	Counter Clockwise
CCZ	Coastal Confluence Zone
CD	Chart Datum
CD	Compact Disc
CDC	Centre for Disease Control
CDC	Central Distribution Center
CDC	Clean Diesel Combustion
CDC	Continuous Discharge Certificate
CDG	Carriage of dangerous Goods

CDGCPL2	Classification of dangerous Goods
CDG Rail	Carriage of dangerous Goods By Rail
CDLSE	Clearance Divers Life Support Equipment
CDP	Controlled Depletion Polymers
CD-ROM	Compact Disk-Read Only Memory
CDW	Collision Damage Waiver
CDT	Central daylight Time
CER	Carriage of Explosive Regulations
CEPT	Conference Of European Telecommunication Administration
CER	Carriage of Explosives Regulations
CET	Central European Time
CET	Common External Tariff
CFBP	Crime & Fraud Prevention Bureau(insurance)

CFBR	Custom Freight Business Review
CFC	Chlorofluorocarbon
CFC	Community of fisheries control
CFC	Consolidation Freight Classification
CFD	Computational Fluid Dynamics
CFO	Chief Financial Officer
CFR	Code of Federal Regulation
CFS	Container Freight Station
CET	Common External Tariff
CF	Cost and Freight
CFS	Container Freight Station
CFSP	Custom Freight Simplified Procedure
CG	Center of Gravity
CG	Coast Guard
CG	Consumer Goods

CGA	Compressed Gas Association
CGL	Commercial General Liability
CGSA	Carriage of Goods By Sea Act
CGT	Compensated Gross Tonnage
CGT	Cummins Generator Technologies
CE	Chronometer Error-Compass Error
CEDEX	Container Equipment Data Exchange
CEMA	Conveyor Equipment Manufacturers' Association
CEMA	Customs and Excise Management Act
CEMEC	European Center for Disaster Management
CEP	Circular Probable Error
CES	Coast Earth Station
CFC	Consolidation freight Classification
CFR	Code of Federal Regulations

CGPM	Conference General Des Poids ET Mesures
CGPM	General Conference of Weights & Measures
CGT	Compensated Gross Tonnage
CH	Compass Heading
CHANs	Chemical Hazard Alert Notices
CHEM	Container Handling Equipment Manufacturer's Association
CHIEF	Customs Handling of Import & Export Freight
CHIRPS	Chemicals, Hazard Information & Packing for Supply
CHIRP	Confidential Human Incident Reporting Program
CHMM	Certified Hazardous Materials Manager
CIA	Cash In Advance

CIC	Container Inspection Criteria
CIE	Captain's Imperfect Entry
CIE	International Commission on Illumination
CIF	Carriage, Insurance & Freight
CIF	Charged In Full (custom duty)
CIF&C	Cost, Insurance, Freight, and Commission
CILT	Chartered Institute of Logistic & Transport
CIPM	Commission Internationale de Poids et megures
CJR	Commodity Jurisdiction Request
CLER	The Classification & labeling of Explosive Regulation
CLI	Call Line Identification
CME	Compliance Monitoring & Enforcement

CMG	Course Made Good
CMI	Comite Maritime International
CMS	Constantly Manned Station
CNG	Compressed Natural Gas
CNIS	Channel Navigation Information Service
CO	Cash Order
CO	Chief Officer
COA	Course Of Advance
COC	Chamber of Commerce
COD	Cash on Delivery
COD	Chemical Oxygen Demand
COE	Committee On ECDIS
COFC	Container-On-Flat-Car
COFI	Committee on Fisheries
CoG	Center of Gravity

COG	Course Over Ground
COGAG	Combined Gas & Gas Turbine
COGSA	Carriage of Goods By Sea Act
COL	Cost of Living
COO	Chief Operating Officer
COOC	Contract With Oil or Other Cargo
COP	Custom Of Port
COS	Cash on Shipment
COS	Chief of Staff
COSAG	Combined Steam Turbine & Gas Turbine
COSMOS	Cost Survey Marine Observation System
COSPAS	Space system for search of distress vessel
COSTGT	Combined Steam Turbine and Gas Turbine
COT	Customer's Own Transport

COW	Crude Oil Washing
COZI	Communication Zone Indicator
CP	Cardinal Point
CPA	Closest Point Of Approach
CPA	Contract Price Adjustment
CPA	Critical Path Analysis
CPA	European Insurance Committee
CPE	Circular Probable Error
CPFF	Cost Plus Fixed Fee
CPI	Consumer Price Index
CPM	Copies Per Minute
CPO	Cancel Previous Order
CPOF	Capacity Planning Using Overall Factor
CPT	Carriage Paid To
CPT	Confederation of Passenger Transport

CPT	Critical Path Technique
CPU	Central Packaging Unit
CR	Carrier's Risk
CPU	Central Processing Unit
CD	Civil Defense
CD	Compact Disc
CDT	Central Daylight Time
CG	Centre of Gravity
CI	Certificate of Insurance
CI	Cast Iron
CICS	Customer Information Control System
CIP	Carrier Identification Parameter
CIP	Carriage & Insurance Paid to (insurance)
CIP	Channel Interface Processor
CIP	Customer Identification Program

CIP	Controlled Insurance Program
CIS	Charts Information System
CISCO	Commercial & Industrial Security Corporation
CISCO	Council Of International Shipping Consultant
CISCO	Computer Information System Company
CL	Clearance
CMC	Chamber of Maritime Commerce
CMC	Central Maintenance Computer
CMC	Conditional Moment Closure
CMC	Crises Management Center
CMD	Cummins MerCruiser Diesel Marine
CMG	Course Made Good
COA	Course of Advance
COC	Chief Officer Certificate

COD	Cash On Delivery
COD	Chemical Oxygen Demand
COE	Committee on ECDIS (IHO)
COG	Course over Ground
COHMED	Co-operative Hazardous Material Enforcement Development
CP	Center of Pressure
CPA	Closest point of Approach
CPC	Certificate Of Professional Competence
CPE	Circular Probable Error
CPP	Controllable Pitch Propeller
CPR	Cardiac Pulmonary Resuscitation
CPSC	Certificate of Proficiency In Survival Craft
CPT	Curriculum Practical Training

CPT	Carriage Paid To (insurance)
CPT	Comprehensive Performance Test
CPT	Confederation of Passenger Transport
CPU	Central Processing Unit
CQR	Chatham Quick Release
CR	Carrier Risks
CRS	Coast radio Station
CRT	Cathode- Ray tube
CS	Classification Society
CSC	International Convention for Safe Container
CSEU	Confederation of Shipbuilding & Engineering Union
CSH	Continuous Survey Hull
CSI	Critical Safety Index

CSM	Continuous Survey Machinery
CSP	Commencement Search Pattern
CSS	Cargo Stowage and Securing
CSS	Coordinator Surface Search
CSS	Control Stick Steering
CSS	Contingency Support Staff
CSS	Communication System Segment
CSS	Computer Search System
CSS	Common System Software
CSW	Code of Safe Working Practice
CT	Combined Transport
CT	Conference Terms
CTO	Chief Technical Officer
CTO	Combined Transport Operator
CTP	Common Transport Policy

CTU	Cargo Transport Unit
CTV	Color Television
CTZ	Control Traffic Zone
CUS	Chassis Usage Surcharge
CV	Curriculum Vitae
CVC	Code Verification Certificate
CVC	Combustible Vapor Concentration
CVC	Customer Value Contract
CVK	Central Vertical Keel
CW	Commercial Weight
CW	Continuous Wave
CWE	Cleared Without Examination
CWO	Cash With Order
CY	Calendar Year
CY	Container Yard

CZ	Canal Zone
CZAM	Coastal Zone Management Act
CZn	Compass Azimuth

D

D	Deviation; Dip, Distance
DA	Driver Accompanied
DAC	Digital-to-Analog Converter
DAF	Delivered At Frontier (insurance)
DAN	Delivery Advice Note
DASD	Direct Access Storage Device (computer)
DAT	Double Acting Tank
DAT	Drug & Alcohol Test
DAT	Delivered at Terminal

DAT	Direct Access Trading
DAP	Directory Access Protocol
DAP	Digital Audio Player
DAP	Digital Auto Pilot
DAP	Data Analysis Program
DAP	Delivered at Place
DAP	Digital Audio Processor
DB	Double Bottom
DBMS	Database Management System
DC	Document Against Cash
DC	Direct Current/Distribution Center
DCC	Digital Compact Cassette
DCU	Data Collection Unit
DD	Dry Dock
DD	Dishonorable Discharge

DDP	Delivered Duty Paid
DDP	Disc Description Protocol
DDP	Deep Down Production
DDP	Declaration of Design and Performance
DDP	Defect Detection and Prevention
DB	Double bottom
DC	Direct current
DCU	Data Collection Unit
DCW	Dead Carcass Weight
DD	Damage Done (insurance)
DD	Double Deck/Damage Done (insurance)
DDE	Direct Data Entry
DDI	Data/Direct Dialing Inward (communication)

DDO	Dispatch Payment on Discharge Only
DDP	Delivered Duty Paid (insurance)
DDU	Delivered Duty Unpaid (insurance)
DE	Design & Equipment
DEG	Degree (metrology)
DEMU	Diesel Electric Multiple Unit
DES	Delivered Ex Ship (insurance)
DEQ	Delivered Ex-Quay (insurance)
DETR	Department of Environment, Transport and the Regions
DEW	Distance Early Warning
Df	Draft Forward
DFIEM	Diesel Fuel Injection Equipment Manufacturers
DG	Directional Gyro
DGAC	Dangerous Goods Advisory Council

DGPS	Differential Positioning System
DGN	Dangerous Goods Notes
DGR	Dangerous Goods Regulations
DGSA	Dangerous Goods Safety Advisor
DH	Double Hull
DHQ	Mean Diurnal High Water Inequality
DI	Delivery Instructions
DIC	Delivery In Charge
DIN	Deutches Institute Fur Normung
DISH	Data Intercharge for Shipping
DLQ	Mean Diurnal Low water inequality
DLQ	Deck Landing Qualification
DMA	Direct Memory Access (computer)
DMAHTC	Defense Mapping Agency Hydrographic/Topographic Centre

DMB	Datum Marker Buoy
DME	Distance Measuring Equipment
DMU	Diesel Multiple Unit
DNC	Digital Navigational chart
DNV	Det Norske Veritas
DOA	Dead On Arrival
DOB	Date of Birth
DOC	Document Of Compliance
DOE	Department of Environment
DOP	Dilution Of Precision
DOS	Disc Operating System
DOSV	Deep Ocean Survey Vehicle
DOT	Department Of Transportation
DP	Dynamic Position /Departure Point
DPA	Designated Person Ashore

DPO	Dynamic Position Officer
DPP	Deferred Payment Plan
DPS	Dynamic Positioning/planning System
D.R	Dead Reckoning; Dead Reckoning Position
DRAW	Direct Read After Write (computer)
DRE	Dead Reckoning Equipment
DRI	Direct Reduced Iron
DRM	Direction of Relative Movement
DRT	Dead Reckoning Tracer
DS	Data set
DSC	Data Source Control
DSC	Digital Selective Calling
DSC	Digital Scan Converter
DSC	Digital Still Camera

DSC	Direct Satellite Communication
DSC	Driver Safety course
DSC	Dual Supply Control
DSC	Dynamic Stability Control
DSC	Dynamically Supported Craft
DSHA	Dangerous Substances In Harbors & Harbors Areas
DSME	Daewoo Shipbuilding and Marine Engineering
DST	Daylight Saving
DSV	Deep sea Vessel
DSV	Diving Support Vessel
DSV	Dynamic Supply vessel
DSVL	Double Second Difference
DBS	Direct Broadcasting by Satellite
DDD	Direct Distance Dialing

DIN	Data Identification Number
DMT	Disaster Management team
DOA	Dead On Arrival
DOD	Department of Defense
DOM	Date Of Marriage
DOS	Disk Operating System
DP	Displaced Person
DSL	Digital Subscriber Lined
DTI	Department of Trade and Industry
DTP	Desk-top publishing
DV	Desired Value
DW	Dock Water
DWA	Dock Water Allowance
DX	Long-Distance Telecommunications
DXF	Data Exchange Format

DYB	Do Your Best
DYD	Dockyard
DZ	Delivery Zone

E	East
EA	Environmental Agency
EASA	European Aviation Safety Authority
E&OE	Errors & Omissions Expected
EAT	Expected Approach Time
EAM	Enterprise Assets Management
EBL	Electronic Bearing Line
EBM	Electronic Bearing Marker
EBRD	European Bank For Re construction & development

EBS	Emergency Bunker Surcharge
EC	Electronic Chart
EC	European Community
ECA	Emission Controlled area
ECBL	European Certification Boards for Logistics
ECD	Envelope to Cycle Difference
ECDB	Electronic Chart Data Base
ECDIS	Electronic Chart Display & Information System
ECE	Economic Commission for Europe
ECH	English Channel
ECHR	European Court of Human Rights
ECMWF	European Center for Medium-Range Weather Forecasting
ECOSOC	Economic & Social Council

ECR	Engine Control Room
ECR	Electronic Cash Register
ECS	Electronic Charting System
ECU	Electric Control Unit
ED	Existence Doubtful
EDC	Error Detection and Correction
EDD	Estimated Date of Departure
EDG	Emergency Diesel Generator
EDH	Efficient deckhand
EDI	Electronic Data Interchange
EDP	Electric Data Processing
EDR	Equipment Damage Report
EEBD	Emergency Escape Breathing Device
EEC	European Economic Market
EEDI	Emergency Efficiency Design Index

EEFAH	Maximum distance between Ends of Fore & Aft Holds
EEMP	Envoy Extraordinary & Minister Plenipotentiary
EEO	Equal Employment Opportunity
EET	Eastern European Time
EEZ	Exclusive Economic Zone
EFSWR	Extra Flexible Steel Wire Rope
EFTS	Electronic Funds Transfer System
EGPA	Egyptian General Petroleum Authority
EGC	Enhanced Group Calling
EGNO	European Geostationary Navigation Overlay System
EGR	Exhaust Gas Recirculation System
EGS	Electronic Guide System
EHA	Equipment Handover Agreement

EHF	Extreme High Frequency
EIA	Environmental Impact Assessment
EHIC	European Health Insurance Card
EIB	European Investment Bank
EIR	Environment Information Regulations
EIS	Environmental Impact Assessment
ELC	European Logistic Centre
ELD	Economic Load Distribution
ELECTRA M	Enforcement Liaison Committee on the Safe Transport of Radio Active Materials
ELR	Export Licensing Regulations
ELSIE	Electronic Signaling & Indicating Equipment
ELT	Emergency Locator Transmitter
ELV	Exposure Limit Value
ELWS	Extreme Low-Water Level Spring Tide

EM	Electro Magnetic
EMAD	Engine Maintenance & Disassembly
EMC	Electromagnetic Compatibility
EMCOF	European Monitory Cooperation Fund
EMF	Electromotive Force
EMS	Enhanced Message Service
EMS	Environmental Management System
EMSA	European Maritime Safety Agency
EMU	Economic & Monitory Union
EN	European Standard Norm/Number
ENC	Electronic Navigational chart
ENCDB	Electronic Navigation Chart Data Base
ENP	Electronic Number Plate
ENS	Electronic Navigation System
EOM	End of Month

EOP	Emergency Operating Procedures
EOT	End of Transmission
EP	Estimated Position
EPC	Engineering, Procurement & Construction Project
EPE	Estimated Position Error
EPIRP	Emergency Position- Indicating Radio Beacon
ELC	Environment Liaison Centre
ELT	Emergency Locator transmitter
EMA	European-Mediterranean Seismological Centre
EMC	Electromagnetic Compatibility
ENC	Electronic Navigation Chart
ENS	Electric Navigational System
EOQC	European Organization for Quality Control

EPA	Environmental Protection Agency
EPE	Estimated Position Error
EPG	Emergency Procedures Guidelines
EPIRP	Emergency Position Indicating Radio Beacon
EPROM	Erasable Programmable Read Only Memory
EPS	Expanded Polystyrene (packing)
EQUIP	Equipment Usage Information Program
ER	Emergency Room
ERG	Emergency Response Guide Book
ERROM	Erasable & Programmable Read Only memory
ERTIS	European Road Transport
ES	Environment System

ESA	Employment service Agency
ESB	Employment & Skills Board
ESD	Emergency Shutdown Device
ESM	Executive Ship Management
ESP	Event Stock Planning
ESP	Electronic Stability Programming
ESPD	Export Service & Promotions Division
ESPRIT	European Strategic Program for Research & Information
ESSA	Environmental Science Services Administration
ESV	Earth Satellite Vehicle
ET	Ephemeris Time/Eastern Time
ETA	Estimated Time of Arrival
ETD	Electronic Transfer of Data
ETD	Estimated Time of Departure

ETE	Estimated Time En route
ETI	Estimated Time of Interception
ETO	European Transport Organization
ETV	Emergency Towing Vessel
EU	European Union
EXS	Ex-ship
EXW	Ex-Work
EZC	European Zone Charge

F

F	Fahrenheit;Fast
FA	First Aid
FA	Fair average Quality of Season
FAA	Federal Aviation Authority
FAA	Free of All Average (insurance)

FAC	Forwarding/Freight Agents Commission
FAK	Freights All Kinds
FAP	Free of Particular Average
FAQ	Fair Average Quality
FAQ	Free Alongside
FAQ	Frequently Asked Question
FAR	For Accidents Reporting
FAS	Free Alongside Ship (Insurance)
FAS	Fire Alarm System
FAS	Fetal Alcohol Syndrome
FAS	Federation of Astronomical Society
FAS	Fuel Automated System
FAS	Fueling at Sea
FAS	Financial analysis system

FAS	Fleet Attack Submarine
FAS	Financial Accounting Service
FAST	First Atomic Ship Transport
FAST	First Automatic Shuttle Transfer
FB	Freight Bill
FBH	Fire Brigade Hydrant
FBF	Freight Forwarders Combined Transport Bill of Lading
FC	Fund Convention
FCA	Full Cost Accounting
FCA	Free Carrier (insurance)
FCA	Formal Concept Analysis
FCA	Full Cost Accounting
FCAR	Free of Claim for Accident Reported
FCC	Federal Communication Commission

FCC	Freight Consolidating Center
FCFS	First Come First Served
FCI	Freight Carriage and Insurance
FCL	Full Container Load
FCP	Fatigue-Crack Propagation (engineering)
FCP	Freight Carriage Paid (commercial)
FCR	Forwarder's Certificate of Receipt
FCS	Fleet Communication System
FCT	Forwarder's Certificate of Transport
FDA	Food & Drug Administration
FDD	Freight Demurrage Dispatch
FDF	Food and Drink Federation (manufacturing)
FDR	Fuel Duty Rebate (transport)
FEC	Forward Error Correction

FEUS	Forty-Foot Equivalent Unit
FFA	Fire Fighting Appliance
FFI	For Further Instructions
FFL	Fixed and Flashing
FE	Far East
FH	Fire Hydrant
FIC	Flight Information Centre
FIFA	Federation of International Football Association
FIFO	First- In, First-Out(stock Control)
FILO	First-In, Last-Out (stock control)
FIOA	Freedom of Information Act
FIOS	Free In and Out Stowed
FIOT	Free In/Out & Training
FITS	Future Intelligent Transport System

FIUO	For Internal Use Only
FLIR	Forward Looking Infra-Red
FLT	Foreign Language Test
FLT	Fork Lift Truck
FM	Frequency Modulation
FM	Full Moon
FM	Fish Meal
FM	Formal Method
FM	Facility Module
FMA	Failure Mode Analysis
FMC	Federal Marine Commission
FMC	Flexible Machine Center
FMCG	Fast Moving Customer Goods(commercial)
FMECA	Failure Mode Effective Critical Analysis

FMF	Fleet Marine Force
FMS	Flexible Manufacturing System
FMS	Freight Management System
FNO	Fleet Navigation Officer
F.O	Fuel Oil/Free Out
FOB	Free On Board
FOC	Flag Of Convenience
FOC	Free Of Charge
FOC	Free Of Claims
FOC	Full Operation Capability
FOD	Free Of Damage
FOD	Foreign Object Damage
FOI	Freedom Of Information
FONASBA	Federation of National Associations of Shipbrokers & Agents

FOP	Form Of Payment
FOQ	Free On Quay
FOR	Free On Rail
FOREX	Foreign Exchange
FORS	Freight Operator Recognition Scheme
FORTRAN	Formula Translation (computer)
FOS	Free On Ship/Station
FOSC	Fleetwood Offshore Survival Centre
FOSC	Federal On-Scene Commander
FOT	Free On Truck
FOT	Free Of Tax
FOT	Fiber Optic Transceiver
FOT	Follow-On Training
FOW	First Open Water

FP	Flash Point
FP	Floating Policy
FP	Fully Paid
FPA	Fire Protection Association
FPA	Free of Particular Average
FPAD	Freight Payable At Destination
FPO	Fire Prevention Officer
FPSO	Floating Production Storage Offloading System
FPV	Fisheries Protection Vessel
FQP	Freight Quality Partnership
FR	Fixed Route
FRC	Fast Rescue Craft
FRD	Forward
FRN	Floating Rate Note (finance)

FRO	Fire Risk Only (insurance)
FRS	Fixed Route Schedule
FSE	Free service Effect
FSI	Flag State Implementation
FSK	Frequency Shift Key
FSMs	Free Surface Moments
FSIRG	Fluid Structure Interaction Research Group
FSO	Fire Safety Officer
FSO	Floating Storage and Offloading
FSR	Free of Strikes, and Riots (insurance)
FSRU	Floating Storage Regasification Unit
FSRV	Floating Storage Regasification Vessel
FSU	Floating Storage Unit
FSV	Fast Supply Vessel

FSV	Fuel Shut-off Valve
FSW	Friction Stir Welding
FSWR	Flexible Steel Wire Rope
FTA	Freight Transport Association
FTA	Free Trade Area (agreement)
FTC	Fast Time Constant
FTC	Freight Transshipment Center
FTC	Freight Transportation Cost
FTE	Full Time Equivalent
FTL	Full Tanker Load
FTP	Fire Test Procedures
FTW	Free Trade Wharf
FTZ	Free-Trade Zone
FU	Follow Up
FUF	First Updated Forecast (manufacturing)

FUQ	Flexible Vocational Qualification
FVO	Fleet View online Service
F.W	Fresh Water
FWA	Fresh Water Allowance
FWC	Full Weight and Capacity
FWE	Finished With Engine
FWL	Full Wagon Load
FWT	Fear Wear and Tear
FX	Foreign Exchange
FY	Fiscal Year
FYP	Five-Year Plan
FZRA	Freezing Rain

G

G	Greenwich; Grid
GAPA	Ground-to-Air Pilotless Aircraft
GATT	General Agreement on Tariffs & Trade
GAT	Greenwich Apparent Time
GB	Great Britain
GB	Grid Bearing
GBD	Grievous Bodily Harm
GBP	Global Ballast Partnership
GCBS	General Council of British Shipping
GCC	Gulf Cooperation Council
GCW	Gross Combination Weight
GEBO	General Bathymetric Charts of the Ocean

GEF	Global Environment Facility
GEO	Geostationary Earth Orbit
GEOLUT	Geo-Sat system Local User Terminal
GEOSAR	Geo-satellite System for SAR
GES	Ground Earth Station
GFCM	General Fisheries Council for the Mediterranean
GFMVT	General Food Moisture Vapor Test
GHA	Greenwich Hour Angle
GHG	Green House Gas
GHQ	General Headquarters
GHS	Global Harmonizing System
GIA	Global Industry Alliance
GISIS	Global Integrated Shipping Information System
GIT	Goods In Transit

GLERL	Great Lakes Environment Research Laboratory
GLO	Group Litigation Order (legal)
GLONASS	Global Orbiting Navigation Satellite System
GLP	Good laboratory Practice
GLS	General Logistic System
GLT	Gas To Liquid (fuel technology)
GLW	Gross Laden Weight
GM	Metacentric Height
GM	Germanischer Lloyd
GM	Guided Missile
GM	General Manager
GmBH	German wording: Private Limited Company
GMCF	Global Mobile Commerce Forum

GMDSS	Global Maritime Distress & Safety System
GMEF	Global Ministerial Environment Forum
GMMO	Genetically Modified Micro-Organism
GMO	Genetically Modified Organism
GMP	Good Manufacturing Processes
GMR	Goods Movements Reporting
GMP	Garbage Management Plan
GMST	Greenwich Mean Sidereal Time
GMT	Greenwich Mean Time
GMW	Gram Molecular Weight
GND	Ground (meteorology)
GNOR	Grounded Non-Operational for Repair
GNSS	Global Navigation Satellite Systems

GO	Government Office
GOES	Geostationary Operational Environmental Satellite
GOES	Global Omnibus Environmental Survey
GOH	Goods On Hanger
GPD	Gallons Per Day
GPH	Gallons Per Hour
GPM	Gallons Per Minute
GPO	General Post Office
GPRS	General Packet Radio Service
GPS	Gallons per Second
GPS	Gas Pressure Switch
GPS	General Purpose Segment
GPS	Global Positioning System
GPS	Global Product Support

GPS	Ground Processing System/station
GRB	Garbage Record Book
GRI	Group Repetition Interval
GRM	Gravity Research Mission
GRN	Goods Received Note
GRP	Glass Reinforcement Plastic
GRT	Gross Registered Tonnage
GS	General Staff
GS	Ground Speed
GSAT	General Security Awareness Training
GSD	General Supply depot
GSE	Ground Service Equipment
GSF	Gross Square Feet
GSLP	Guaranteed Student Loan Program
GSM	Global System for Mobiles

GSP	Generalized System of Preferences (customs)
GSP	Glass Strengthen Polyester
GST	Greenwich Sidereal Time
GT	Gross Tonnage/Gas Turbine
GTIN	Global Trade Item number
GTL	Gas To Liquid
GTM	Global Transportation Management
GTS	Gas Turbine Ship
GTTS	Global Transport telematics System
GTW	Gross Trailer Weight
GV	Grid Variation
GVM	Gross Vehicle Mass
GVTS	Goods Vehicle Testing Station
GWP	Global Warming Potential

GWP	Global Water Partnership
GWP	Gross World Production
GWP	Gross Written Premium
GZ	Ship Righting Lever

<u>H</u>

H	Hour
HCL	High Cost of Living
HCWM	High Capacity Washing Machine
HD	Heavy Duty
HDI	Human Development Index
HDLC	High Level Data Link Control
HDOP	Horizontal Dilution of Precession
HE	Height of Eye
HE	Heeling Error

HEX	Hexagonal
HF	High Frequency
HFC	Hydrofluoricarbon
HFO	Heavy fuel Oil
HHW	Higher High Water
HHWI	Higher High Water Interval
H/L	Heavy Lift
HLA	Helicopter Landing Area
HLO	Helicopter Landing Officer
HLW	High Low Water
HLWI	High Low Water Interval
HMI	Human Machine Interface
HNS	Hazardous & Noxious Substances
HP	High Performance
HP	High Pressure

HP	High Profile
HP	High Priority
HP	Horizontal parallax
HP	Horse Power
HPFWW	High Pressure Fresh Water Wash
HRA	High Risk Area
HRD	Human Resources Development
HRN	House Recovery Net
HRU	Hydrostatic Release Unit
HSC	High Speed Craft
HSD	High Speed Data
HSE	Health and Safety Executive
HSGT	High Speed Ground Transport
HSPA	High Speed Packet Access
HSPA	High Speed Parallel Adder

HSSC	Harmonized System of Survey and Certification
HT	Half Time
HT	High Tension
HIV	Header Isolation Valve
HIV	High Interest Vessel
HIV	Human Immune Deficiency Virus
HRD	Human Resources Development
HVAC	High Voltage Alternating current
HW	High Water
HWF&C	High Water Full & Change
HWI	High Water Interval
HWQ	Tropic High Water Inequity
HWS	Hurricane Warning System
Hzy	Hazy (meteorology)

I

I	Instrument Correction
IACS	International Association of Classification Societies
IAEA	International Atomic Energy Agency
IAF	International Astronautical Federation
IALA	International Association of Lighthouse Authorities
IAM	International Association of Meteorology
IAMSAR	International Aeronautical &Marine Search &Rescue Manual
IAP	International Airport
IAP	Internet Access Provider (Web)
IAPH	International Association of Ports and Harbors

IARW	International Association of Refrigerated Warehouses
IATA	International Air Transport Association
IAU	International Astronautical Union
IAU	International Astronomical Union
IBC	International Bulk Chemical Code
IBM	Integrated Business Management
IBM	Industrial Business Machine Corporation(US company)
IBM	Initial Body Mass
IBS	Integrated Bridge System
IBTS	Integrated Bilge Water Treatment
IBWM	International Bureau of Weights & Measures
IC	Index Correction/Internal combustion

ICAA	International Civil Aviation Authority
ICAN	International Commission for Air Navigation
ICAO	International Civil Aviation Organization
ICB	International Container Bureau
ICC	Inter-Conference Committee
ICC	International Chamber of Commerce
ICCS	Integrated Coastguards Communication System
ICE	In Case of Emergency
ICJ	International Court of Justice
ICS	Institute of Chartered Shipbrokers
ICS	International Chamber of Shipping
ICT	Information & Communication technology

ICT	International Combined Transport
ICU	Intensive Care Unit
ICW	Intracoastal Waterway
ID	Identity or Identification
IDD	International direct Dialing
IDDD	International Direct Distance Dialing
IDL	International Date Line
IDL	International driving License
IDLH	Immediately Dangerous to Life & Health
IDP	International Driving Permit
I.E	Index Error
IEC	International Electro technical Commission
IF	Intermediate Frequency
IFAD	International Fund for Agricultural Development

IFB	Invitation For Bid
IFCC	Internet Fraud Complaint Centre
IFR	Instrument Flying Rating
IFRB	International Frequency Registration Board
IFSMA	International Federation of Ship's Masters' Association
I.G	Inert Gas/Imperial Gallon
IGS	Inert Gas System
IGLD	International Great Lakes Datum
IHB	International Hydrographic Bureau
IHO	International Hydrographic Organization
IFF	Identification, Friend or Foe
IFO	Identified Flying Object
IFRC	International Federation of Red Cross & Red Crescent Society

IICL	Institute of International Container Lessors
ILO	International Labor Organization
ILS	Integrated Logistic Support
ILS	Instrument Landing System
IMA	Interim Management Association
IMA	Intermediate maintenance Activity
IMARSAT	International Maritime Satellite Organization
IMAS	International Maritime & Shipping Conference
IMC	Instrument Meteorological Condition
IMC	International Maritime Committee
IMCO	International Maritime Consultative Organization
IMDG	International Maritime Dangerous Goods (code)

IMES	Inmarsat Mobile Earth station
IMGS	International Medical Guide for Ship
IMLI	International Marine Law Institute
IMO	International Maritime Organization
IMO	International Meteorological Organization
IMRAN	International Marine Radio Aids to Navigation
IN'CARG	Int. Association of Dry Cargo Owners
INCOTERMS	International Rules for the Interpretation of Trade Terms
INF	Irradiated Nuclear Fuel
INM	International Nautical Mile
INMARSAT	International Mobile Satellite Organization
INS	Integrated Navigation System

INSAT	Indian Geostationary Satellite
IOPPC	International Oil Pollution prevention Certificate
IOU	I Owe You
IPI	Inland Point Intermodal
IPMS	Integrated Platform Management System
IPS	Integrated Power System
IR	Information Retrieval
IRF	Incident Report Form
ISBN	International Standard Book Number
ISM	International Safety Management (code)
ISO	International Standardization Organization
IBMT	Internet-Based Test
ICAO	International Civil Aviation Organization

ICC	International Chamber of Commerce
ICDL	International Computer Driving License
ICES	International Council for the Exploration of the Sea
ICFTU	International Confederation of Free Trade Union
ICND	International Commission on Narcotic Drugs
ICOS	International Committee of Onomastic Sciences
ICAPA	International Commission for the Prevention of Alcoholism
ICRC	International Committee of the Red Cross
ICSU	International Council of Scientific Union
ID	Identity Card

IDDD	International Direct Distance Dialing
IEC	International Electro technical Commission
IFA	International Fiscal Association
IFAD	International Fund for Agricultural Development
IFC	International Finance Corporation
IFF	Identification, Friend, or Foe
IFO	Identified Flying Object
IFRC	International Federation of Red Cross and Red Crescent Societies
IFRC	Int.Fed.of Red Cross & Red Cressent
IFSMA	International Federation of Shipmasters 'Association
IGCSE	International General Certificate of Secondary Education
IHO	International Hydrographic Organization

ILO	International Labor Organization
ILS	Instrument Landing System
IMCA	International Marine Contractor Association
IMF	International Monetary Fund
IMO	Incident Management Office
IMO	Information Management Office
IMO	In My Opinion
IMO	International Maritime Organization
IMO	International meteorological Organization
IMO	Internet Mail Only
IMO	International Money Order
IMP	Integrated Maritime Policy
IMLI	International Maritime Law Institute
INCB	International Narcotics Control Board

INDEX	Institute for Nano electronics Discovery and Exploration
INDEX	Institutional Data Exchange
INEX	International Nuclear Emergency Exercise
INM	International Nautical Mile
INMARSAT	International Maritime Satellite Organization
INS	Inertial Navigation System
INTACT	Integrated Telematics for Advanced Communications In
	Freight Transport
INTANKO	International Association of Independent Tank Owners
INTERCO	International Code Of Signal
INTERPOL	International Criminal Police Commission

INTIS	International Transport & Information System
IOC	International Olympic Committee
IOME	Institute Of Marine Engineering
ION	Institute Of Navigation
IOT	Institute Of Transport
IOU	I Owe You
IOV	In-Orbit Validation (satellite Navigation)
IP	Internet Protocol (Web)
IPA	International Phonetic Alphabet
IPAA	International Petroleum Association of America
IPPC	Integrated Pollution Prevention & Control
IQ	Interrupted Quick Flashing
IR	Interference Rejection
IRC	Internet Relay Chat

IRCS	Ship borne Integrated Radio Communication System
IRO	International Refugee Organization
IRP	Image-retaining Panel
IRPTC	International Register of Potentially Toxic Chemicals
ISBN	International Standard Book Number
ISD	International Subscriber Dialing
ISDN	Integrated Service Digital Network
ISF	International Shipping Federation
ISG	Industry Steering Group
ISGOT	International Safety Guide for Oil Tankers & Terminals
ISI	Information Society Initiative
ISIS	International Shipping Information Services

ISLW	Indian Spring Low Water
ISM	International Safety Management
ISO	International Standardization Organization
ISP	Internet Service Provider
ISPS	International Port Facility Security (Code)
ISU	International Seaman's Union
ISWG	International standardWire Gauge
ITF	International Transport Federation
ITM	Institute of Transport Management
ITM	Integrated Transport Management
ITO	International Trade Organization
ITP	Intercept Terminal Point
ITS	Integrated Transport System

ITS	International Temperature Scale
ITSA	Independent Tank Storage Association
ITT	Invitation To Tender
ITU	Intermodal transport Unit
ITU	International Telecommunication Union
IU	International Unit
IUC	International Union for the Conservation of Nature
IUGG	International Union of Geodesy & Geophysics
IUM	International Union of Marine Insurance
IUMI	International Union of Maritime Insurers
IUQ	Interrupted Ultra Quick Flashing
IVQ	Interrupted Very Quick Flashing

IW	Index Words
IWD	Inland Waterways and Docks
IWG	Imperial Wire Gauge
IWM	Institute of Wastes Management
IWS	In Water Survey
IWTA	Inland Water Transport Association
IWW	Intracoastal Waterway
IYC	International Yacht Collection

J

JA	Joint Account
JAA	Joint Aviation Authorities
JAL	Japan Airline
JCCC	Joint Customs Consultative Committee
JD	Justice Department

JD	Juvenile Delinquent
JETCO	Japan Export Trading Company
JECFI	Joint Expert Committee on Food Irradiation
JIC	Just In Case
JIU	Joint Inspection Unit
JNCC	Joint Nature Conservation Committee
JP	Jet Propelled (Engine)
JPS	Jet Propelled System
JRC	Japan Radio Company
JRC	Joint Rescue Coordinator
JTC	Joint Training Committee
JTL	Just Too Late
JV	Joint Venture
JWG	Joint Working Group

K

K	Kelvin (measurement)
KB	Knowledge Base
KBES	Knowledge- Based Expert System
KCT	Klang Container Terminal
KCT	Khor Fakkan Container Terminal
KISS	'Keep It Simple, Sir'/Keep It Short & Simple
Kn	Knot (maritime)
KOD	Kick-Off Drift
KOICA	Korea International Co-operation Agency
KPI	Key Performance Indicator
KPL	Kilometer Per Liter
KSF	Key Success Factor

KUTD	Keep Up-To-Date
KVA	Kilo Volt-Ampere
KWIC	Key Word In Context
KWOC	Key World Out Of Context
KWT	Kuwait(international registration letters)

L	Latitude; Lower Limb correction
LA	Law Altitude
LAFES	Load Acquisition & Freight Exchange System
LAN	Local Apparent Noon
LAN	Local Area Network
LANBY	Large Automatic Navigational Buoy
LBP	Length Between Perpendicular

LC	Letter of Credit
LAIS	Loan Accounting Information System
LAM	Limited Area Model
LAM	Local Area Multicomputer
LAN	Local Area Network
LANBY	Large Automatic Navigational Buoy
LAS	League of Arab States
LASER	Light Amplification by Stimulated Emission of Radiation
LASH	Lighter-Aboard Ship
LAT	Local Apparent Time
LATCC	London Air Traffic Control Centre
LAWN	Local Area Wireless Network (computer)
LBV	Landing Barge Vehicle
LBW	Live Body Weight

LC	Letter of Credit
LC	Lethal Concentration
LCA	Life Cycle Assessment
LCAC	Landing craft Air Cushion
LCB	Longitudinal Centre of Buoyancy
LCC	Life Cycle Cost
LCC	Load Carrying Capability
LCCC	London Construction Consolidation Centre
LCCA	Life Cycle Cost Analysis
LCD	Liquid Crystal Display
LCG	Longitudinal Centre of Gravity
LCL	Less than Container Load
LCL	Less Than Car Load Lot (Commercial)
LCM	Landing Craft Mechanized
LCN	Load Classification Number

LCPI	Logistics Cost Per Item (supply)
LCPL	Logistics Cost Per Line (supply)
LCPO	Logistics Cost Per Order (supply)
LCT	Local Civil Time
LCV	Landing Craft Vessel
LCV	Light Commercial Vehicle
LD	Learning Disability
LD	Lethal Dose
LDC	Less Developed Countries
LDG	List of Dangerous Goods
LDO	Lease-Develop-Operate
LDPE	Low Density Polyethylene
LDZ	Local Delivery Zone
LEC	Low Emissions Certificate (engine)
LED	Light- Emitting Diode

LEL	Lower Explosion Limit
LEO	Low Earth Orbit
LEOLUT	Local User Terminal in LEOSAR System
LEOSAR	Low-Earth Orbiting Search & Rescue (Satellite)
LES	Land Earth Station
LESS	Least-Cost Estimating & scheduling
LEV	Low Emission Vehicle (environment)
LEZ	Low Emission Zone (environment)
LF	Low Frequency
LFBS	Light Fuel Blending Stock
LFD	Late Finished Date
LFDCA	London Fire & Civil Defense Authority
LFL	Lower Flammable Limit
LFL	Low Flashing

LFL	Low Flash Point Liquid
LGV	Large/Light Goods Vehicle
LH	Left Handed
LHA	Local Hour Angle
LHS	Left-Hand Sided
LHV's	Longer and Heavier Vehicles
LHW	Lower High Water
LHWI	Lower High Water Interval
LIBA	Lloyd's Insurance Brokers' Association
LIC	Local Import Control
LIDAR	Laser Infrared Detection& Ranging
LIFO	Last In, First Out
LILO	Last-In, Last-Out (stock)
LIMS	Laboratory Information Management System

LKP	Last Known Position
LL	Lower Limb/ Load Line
LLGDS	Land Locked & Geographically Disadvantaged
LLMC	Limitation of Liability for Marine Claims
LLP	Limited Liability Partnership
LLV	Lunar Logistics Vehicle (astronautics)
LLW	Lower Low Water
LLWD	Lower Low Water Datum
LLWI	Lower Low Water Interval
LMC	Lloyds Machinery Certification ((insurance)
LMC	Last Minute Change
LMIS	Lloyd's Maritime Information Services
LMT	Local Mean Time
LNB	Large Navigational Buoy

LNFE	Low Noise front End
LNG	Liquefied Natural Gas
LNS	Land Navigation System
LNS	Large Neighborhood Search
LOA	Length over All
LOB	Line Of Balance (manufacturing)
LOBAL	Long Base Line Buoy
LOBAR	Long Base Line Rader
LOCAE	List of Classified & Authorized Explosive
LOD	Limit Of Detection
LOE	Law-altitude earth orbit
LOF	Lloyds Open Form 1990(salvage agreement)
LOLER	Lifting Operations& Lifting Equipment Regulations
LO-LO	Load On, Load Off/ Lift-On Lift-Off

LOP	Line Of Position
LORAN	Long Range Navigation
LOSS	Large Objects Salvage System
LOT NO	Number issued by customs for a group of products
LOT	Load On Top (Tankers)
LP	Low Pressure
LPC	Lead Partner Country
LPG	Liquefied Petroleum Gas
LPGA	Logistics Performance Gap Analysis
LPGC	Liquefied Petroleum Gas Carrier
LPU	Long Processing Unit
LR	Lloyds' Registry / Loading Rules
LRAT	Long Range Identification and Tracking
LRTP	Long Range Transportation Planning

LSA	Life Saving Appliances
LSA	Logistics Support Analysis
LSA	Low Specific Activity
LSB	Lower Side Band
LSB	Low Surface Brightness
LSI	Large Scale Integration Technology
LSL	Lower Specification Limit
LSP	Logistic Service Provider
LSS	Life Saving Service
LSQ	Live Sequel (meteorology)
LST	Land Ship Transport
LST	Local Sidereal/ Standard Time
LSZ	Limited Speed Zone
LT	Local Time
LTA	Local Transport Authority

LTA	Long Term Agreement
LTA	Lost Time Accident
LTF	Long-Term Fellowship
LTL	Long-Term Lease
LUNCO	Lloyd's Underwriters Non-Marine Claims Office
LUT	Local User Terminal
LVL	Less Than Vehicle Load
LW	Low Water/ Light Weight
LWD	Low Water Datum
LWI	Low Water Interval
LWL	Load waterline
LWL	Length at Water Line
LWM	Low Water mark
LWONT	Low Water ordinary Neap Tides

LWOST	Low Water ordinary Spring Tides
LWQ	tropic Low Water Inequality
LWR	Least Work Remaining
LZ	Landing Zone

M

M	Meridian; Magnetic; Metacenter
MA	Mechanical Advantage
MAA	Motor Agents Association
MAB	Man Aboard Ship
MACE	Multipurpose Automatic Control Equipment
MAD	Mean Absolute Deviation (statistic)
MAEE	Marine Aircraft Experimental Establishment
MAIB	Marine Accidents Investigation Branch

MARAD	US Maritime Administration
MARCODE	Database of Investigated Accidents
MARPOL	Marine Pollution (convention)
MARS	Meteorological Automatic Reporting Station
MAT	Marine Aviation and Transport
MATS	Military Air Transport Service
MaTSU	Marine Technology Support Unit
MAV	Multi Activity Vehicle
MAWP	Maximum Allowable Working Pressure
MB	Magnetic Bearing
MBU	Making Better Use
MBU	Market-based measures
MBWA	Management By Wandering Around (commercial)

MC	Magnetic Course/ Morse Code
MCA	Maritime &Coastguard Agency
MCC	Mid- Course Correction
MCC	Mission Control Center
MC&G	Mapping & Charting & Geodesy
MCP	Maritime Cargo Processing
MCPA	Minutes to the Closest Point of Approach
MCT	Mean Change of Trim
MCTC	Moment to Change Trim 1 Centimeter
MD	Map distance
MDC	More Developed Countries
MDHB	Mersey Docks & Harbors Board
MDHS	Methods for Determination Hazardous Substances
MDO	Marine Diesel Oil

MDR	Minimum Daily Requirements
ME	Mechanical Engineer/ Marine Engineer
MEA	Marine Exclusive Area
MEC	Marine Evacuation Chute
Medivac	Medical Evacuation
MEGC	Multiple Element Gas Container
MEHRA	Marine Environment High Risk Area
MEPC	Marine Environment Protection Committee
MEL	Maximum Exposure Limit
MEO	Medium Earth Orbit
MEO	Marine Engineering Office
MES	Marine Evacuation System
MET	Meteorological
MEWP	Mobile Elevator Work Platform

MF	Medium Frequency
MFA	Marine Fishing Area
MFAG	Medical First Aid Guide (used with accidents involving DG)
MFC	Motor Fuel Consumption
MFC	Multi-Function Coupling
MFN	Most Favored Nation
MGN	Marine Guidance Notice
MGO	Military Government Ordinance
MH	Medal of Honor/ Magnetic Heading
MHB	Material Hazardous In Bulk
MHR	Mean Hull Roughness
MID	Maritime Identification Digit
MIN	Marine Information Notice
MIP	Marine Insurance Policy

MIIDS	Military Intelligence Integrated Data System
MLB	Mini Land Bridge
MLIT	Ministry of Land, Infrastructure Transport
MLLW	Mean Lower Low Water
MLLW	Mean Lower Low Water Line
MLW	Mean Low Water
MLWL	Mean Lower Water Line
MLWN	Mean Low Water Neap
MM	Materials Management
MM	Multi Modal
MMEL	Master Minimum Equipment List
MMS	Multimedia Message Service
MMSI	Maritime Mobile Service Identity
MMU	Manned Maneuvering Unit

MMU	Memory Management Unit
MN	Mercantile Marine
MNTB	Merchant Navy Training Board
MODU	Mobile Offshore Drilling Unit
MOR	Meteorological Optical Range
MOU	Memorandum Of Understanding
MP	Melting Point
MPCMS	Advanced Machinery Plant Control & Monitoring System
MPCU	Marine Pollution Control Unit
MPL	Maximum Permissible Level
MPL	Mile Per Littre
MPP	Most Probable Position
MRCC	Maritime Rescue Coordinating Centre
MRI	Magnetic Resonance Imaging

MRI	Mean Rise Interval
MRM	Miles of Relative Movement
MRO	Materials Repair & Overhaul
MRU	Mobile Repair Unit
MRV	Multi-Role Vessel
MS	Medical surveillance
MS	Motor Ship
MSB	Maritime Safety Board
MSC	Manchester Ship Canal
MSC	Marine Service Centre
MSC	Maritime Safety Committee
MSC	Maritime Security Council
MSC	Mechanical Speed Control
MSC	Mediterranean Shipping Company
MSC	Message Service Centre

MSC	Meteorological Synthesizing Centre
MSC	Mobile Servicing Centre
MSDS	Material Safety data Sheet
MSG	Meteo-Sat Second Generation (Eumet Sat)
MSI	Maritime Safety Information
MSI	Mass Storage Information
MSI	Multisystem Integration
MSIS	Multi-state Information System
MSL	Mean Sea Level
MSN	Merchant Shipping Notice
MSS	Management Support system
MT	Machine Translator
MT	Mail Transfer
MT	Motor Tanker
MTA	Minimum Terms Agreement

MTCA	Ministry of Transport & Civil Aviation
MTD	Multi Modal Transport Document
MTI	Moving Target Indication
MTL	Mean Tide Level
M.V	Motor Vessel
MVA	Mechanical Vibration Awareness
MW	Mega Watt
MW	Multiple Wave
MW	Medium Wave
MWL	Mean Water Level
MWLL	Mean Water Level Line
MWO	Meteorological Watch Officer
MY	Motor Yacht
MZ	Middle Zone
MZn	Magnetic Azimuth

<u>N</u>

N	Number, North, November
NA	National Academy
NA	Not Applicable/ Not Available
NAA	National Aeronautics Association
NAA	National Automobile Association
NACCAM	National Coordinating Committee for Aviation Meteorology
NAD	North American datum
NADOR	Notification of Accidents& Dangerous Occurrences
NAERA	North American Eastbound Rate Agreement
NAFTA	Newzeland & Australia Free Trade
NAFTA	North American Free Trade Agreement

NANP	No Approach No Photography
NASA	National Aeronautics and Space Administration
NAT	Nordic American Tankers
NATO	North Atlantic Treaty Organization
NATS	Naval Air Transport Service
NAVAR	Navigation and Ranging
NAVINFO NET	Navigation Information Network
NAVSAT	Navigational Satellite
NAVSSI	Navigation Sensor System Interface
NAVSTAR	Navigation System with Time and Ranging
NAVTEX	Navigation Information Transmission System
NAWDC	National Association of Waste Disposal Contractors (UK)

NAWK	National Association of Warehouse Keepers (UK)
NB	Nota Bene
NB	Naval Base
NBDP	Narrow Band Direct Printing
NBS	National Bureau of Standards
NC	No Charges/ Not Changing (meteorology)
NCB	No Claim Bonus (insurance)
NCBAE	No Claim Bonus As earned (insurance)
NCC	National Chemical Carrier
NCC	Network Control Centre
NCEC	National Chemical Emergency Centre
NCF	Navigation Control Facility
NCS	NATO Codification Scheme

NCS	Network Coordination Station
NCV	No Commercial Value
ND	No Date/ Non Delivery
NDB	Non-Directional Beacon
NDC	National Distribution Centre
NDLB	National Dock Labor Board
NDSDTS	National Dangerous Substances Driver Training Scheme
NE	North East
NEA	Nuclear Energy Agency
NEMA	National Marine Electronic Association
NES	Not Elsewhere Specified
NESS	National Earth Satellite Service
NETA	North East Traffic Area
NETT	Network for Environmental Technology Transfer

NFC	National Freight Corporation
NFD	No Fixed Date
NFS	Not For Sale
NFU	Non-Follow Up Mode
NGL	Natural Gas Liquid
NGO	Non-Governmental Organization
NGV	Natural Gas Vehicle
NGVD	National geodetic Vertical datum
NI	Nautical Institute
NIS	Non-Indigenous Species
NLT	Not Less Than
NM	Nautical Mile
NM	Notice to Mariners
NMB	National Maritime Board
NMCH	Non-Methane Hydrocarbons

NMEA	National Marine Electronic Association
NMI	Non-Makeable Interrupt
NMP	New Maintenance Program
NMT	Not More Than
NMU	National Maritime Union
NMW	National minimum Wage
NNE	North-North West
NNF	Not Normally Fitted
NNSS	Navy Navigation Satellite System
NO	Navigation Officer
NOA	Notice Of Arrival
NOAA	National Oceanic & Atmospheric Administration
NOB	Naval Operating Base
NOE	Notice Of Eligibility

NOEC	No Observed Effect Concentration
NOMS	Nuclear Operations Monitoring System
NOS	National Ocean Service
NOS	Network Operating System (computer)
NOS	Not otherwise specified
NP	Notary Public
NP	Nautical Publication
NPD	North Polar Distance
NPM	None-Production Material
NRC	National Research Centre
NRML	New Relative Movement Line
NRO	National Reconnaissance Office
NRT	Net Registered Tonnage
NRV	Non Return Valve
NSA	National Shipping Authority

NSCC	Navigation System Control Centre Satellite
NSCSA	National Company of Saudi Arabia
NSE	National Stock Exchange
NSF	National Science Foundation
NSF	Non Sufficient Fund
NSGU	Navigation Signal Generation Unit
NSSN	National Standard Shipping Note
NT	Neap Tide/ Net Tonnage
NtM	Notice to Mariners
NTDA	National Trade Development Association
NTP	Normal Temperature and Pressure
NUC	Not Under Command
NUMAST	National Union of Marine, Aviation & Shipping Transport
NUS	National Union of Seamen

NVC	Noise and Vibration Comfort
NVD	No Value Declared
NVE	Night Vision Equipment
NVOCC	None-Vessel Operating Common Carrier
NVQ	National Vocational Qualification
NWM	Nuclear Weapon Maneuver
NW	North West
NWS	National Weather Service
NYERDA	New York Energy Research & Developing Authority
NYP	Not Yet Published
NYR	Not Yet Returned
NZ	New Zealand

O

Oc	Occulting (light)
O/A	Over All
OAO	One And Only
OAPEC	Organization of Arab Petroleum Exporting Countries
OAT	Outside Air Temperature
OBO	Oil, Bulk Ore (carrier)
OBU	On-Board Unit
OBV	Ocean Boarding Vessel
OCC	Operations Control Centre
OCIMF	Oil Companies International Marine Forum
OCP	Owners & Contractors Protective Liability Policy

OCR	Optical Character Recognition
OCS	Office of Coast Survey
OCT	Overseas Countries & Territories
OD	Over Draft
ODAS	Oceanographic Data Acquisition Systems
ODP	Ozone Depletion Potential (environment)
OE	Original Equipment
OEC	Over Paid Entry Certificate
OECD	Organization for Economic Co-operation and Development
OEEC	Organization for European Economic Co-operation
OED	Oxford English Dictionary
OEM	Original Equipment Manufacturing Number

OES	Occupational Exposure Standards
OiC	Officer in charge
OIEC	Organization for International Economic Co-operation
OIM	Offshore Installation Manager
OIMOS	Offshore Inland Marine & Oilfield Services
OIT	Office of International Trade
OLB	Official log Book
OMB	Owner-Managed Business
OMB	Office of Management & Budget
OMBO	One Man bridge Operation
ONI	Office of Naval Intelligence
ONR	Office of Naval Research
ONI	Office of Naval Intelligence
ONR	Office of Naval Research

ONWI	Office of Nuclear Waste Isolation
OOD	Officer of the Deck
OOO	Out Of Order
OOW	Officer of the Watch
OP	Observation Post
OP	Open Policy (insurance)
OP	Out of Print
OPA	Oil Pollution Act
OPC	Ordinary Portland Cement
OPEC	Organization of the Exporting Countries
OPIC	Oil Pollution Insurance Certificate
OPIC	Overseas Private Investment Corporation
OPRC	Oil pollution Preparedness, Response, & Cooperation
OR	Owner's Riske

OR	Operating Room
ORB	Oil Record Book
ORV	Off-Road Vehicle
OS	Ordinary Seaman
OSC	On- Scene Commander
OSC	On -Scene Coordinator
OSD	Open Shelter Deck
OSRA	Ocean Shipping Reform Act
OSRO	Oil Spill Removal Organization
OSS	Office of Strategic Service
OST	Offshore Support Tugs
OSV	Offshore Supply Vessel
OSHA	Occupational Safety & Hazardous Health Administration
OSHA	Occupational Safety & Health Administration

OSV	Offshore Support Vessel
OT	Open Top
OT	Overseas Trade
OT	Over Time
OTC	Officer in Tactical Command
OTIU	Overseas Technical Information Unit
OTSR	Optimum Track Ship Routine
OWS	Ocean Weather Service

<u>P</u>

P	Parallax; Polar distance
PA	Particular Average
PA	Position Approximate
P/A	Public Address System
PAB	Person Aboard

PACE	Ports Automated Cargo Environment
PARS	Pre-arrival Review System
PAS	Public Address System
PATRAM	Packing & Transport of Radioactive Materials
PAYE	Pay As You Earn
PBT	Paper-Based Test
PC	Panama Canal
PC	Personal Computer
PC	Personal correction
PCA	Polar Cap Absorption
PCASP	Privately Contracted Armed Security Personnel
PCC	Pure Car Carrier
PCD	Polar Cap disturbance
PCI	Phase Code Interval

PCP	Potential Point of Collision
PCS	Panama Canal Surcharge
PCZ	Panama Canal Zone
PCZST	Panama Canal Zone Standard Time
PD	Position Doubtful
PD	Public Domain
PDA	Personal Digital Assistant
PDA	Predicted Drift Angle
PDD	Polygraph Detection of Deception
PDET	Portable Data Entry Terminal
PDF	Prepared Data Format (computer)
PDI	Pre-Delivery Inspection
PEC	Pilot Exemption Certificate
PEL	Permissible Exposure Limit
PEV	Anti-Piracy Personal Escort Vessel

PF	Personal File
PFC	Per fluorinated Compound
PFEER	Prevention of Fire Explosion & Emergency Response
PG	Post Graduate
PGR	Packaged Goods Regulations
PH	Public Health
PHA	Port Health Authority
PHA	Preliminary Hazard Analysis
PHS	Packing, Handling and Storage
P&I	Protection & Indemnity
PIA	Pakistan International Airline
PILON	Payment In Lieu Of Notice
PIN	Personal Identification Number
PIW	Person In Water
PL	Personal Liability (insurance)

P/L	Position Line
PLB	Personal Locator Beacon
PLC	Product Life Cycle
PLUTO	Pipe-line Under The Ocean
PM	Post-Mortem
PM	Post Meridiem
PM	Pulse Modulation
PML	Probable Maximum Loss (insurance)
PMX	Private Manual Exchange (communication)
PNT	Project Network Techniques
PNYA	Port of New York Authority
PO	Post Office
PO	Pacific Ocean
POA	Power of Attorney
POB	Person ON Board

POB	Place of Birth
POB	Post Office Book
POC	Port Of Call
POD	Pay on Delivery
POD	Port Of Debarkation
POD	Proof Of Delivery
POD	Proof Of Delivery
POE	Point Of Embarkation
POE	Port of Entry
POI	Point Of Interest
POL	Petroleum, Oil & Lubricants
POR	Payable On Return
POR	Payable On Receipt
POSH	Port out, Starboard Home
POST	Point Of Sell Terminal

POV	Point Of View
PP	Pier to Pier
PP	Polypropylene
PPC	Predicted Propagation Correction
PPDP	Point Positioning Data Base
PPE	Personal Protective Equipment
PPI	Plan Position Indicator
PPI	Policy proof on Interest
PPL	Private Pilot's License
PPM	Prints Per Minute
PPM	Public Performance Measure
PPS	Precise Positioning Services
PR	Public Relations
PRAM	Pipeline Risk Assessment Method
PRC	Peoples' Republic of China

PRF	Pulse Repetition Frequency
PR/OBO	Product/Ore-Bulk Oil carrier
PRR	Pulse repletion rate
PRST	Please Return Some Time
PRV	Pressure Relief Valve
PRW	Public Refrigerated Warehouse
PSU	Power Supply Unit
PSV	Platform Supply vessel
PIN	Personal Identification Number
PLC	Public Limited Company
PM	Per Month
PP	Packing Provisions
PPI	Plan Position Indicator
PRN	Pseudo Random Noise
PRO	Public Relation Officer

PRS	Polish Register of Shipping
Ps	Power steering
PSC	Port State Control
PSC&RB	Personal Survival craft & Rescue Boat
PSF	Pound Per Square Foot
PSI	Pounds Per Square Inch
PSI	Proliferation Security Initiative
PSL	Preferred Suppliers List
PSNC	Pacific Steam Navigation Company
PSR	Passenger Service Requirements
PSR	Pipelines Safety Regulations
PSS	Peak Season Surcharge
PST	Pacific Standard Time
PSV	Platform Supply Vessel
PT	Physical Training

PTI	Public Transport Information
PTN	Public Telephone Network
PTO	Please turn Over
PTT	Post, Telegraph & Telephone Administration
PTW	Permit To Work
PTX	Private Trading Exchange
PURV	Powered Underwater Research Vehicle
PV	Pressure Vessel
PV	prime Vertical
PVC	Polyvinyl Chloride
PVT	Pressure, Volume, Temperature
PVV	PIN Verification Values
PWG	Permanent Working Group
PWR	pressurized Water Reactor

PX	Private Exchange (telecommunication)
PYE	Protect Your Environment

<u>Q</u>

Q	Quick Flashing
QA	Quality Assurance
QC	Quality Control
QCP	Quality Control Procedure
QED	Quod Erat Demonestrandum (Which was to be demonstrated)
QF	Quick Firing
QF	Quick Flashing
QFF	Quick Frozen Food
QFT	Qualitative Forecasting Technique
QR	Quick Response

QRP	Quick Response Program
QSHE & S	Quality, Safety, Health, Environment & Security
QVS	Quality Verification Surveillance
QQ	Celestial Equator

R	Refraction
RA	Right Ascension
RACON	Radar Transponder Beacon
RADAR	Radio detection & Ranging
RAF	Royal Air Force
RAIM	Receiver Autonomous Integrity Monitoring (satellite)
RAM	Random-Access Memory
RAM	Reliability, Availability, and Maintainability

RAMP	Rapid Acquisition of Manufactured Parts (purchasing)
RASH	Rain Shower (meteorology)
RASH	Rain and Snow(meteorology)
RATAN	Radar & Television Aid to Navigation
RB	Relative Bearing
RBn	Radio Beacon
RCC	Recovery Control center
RCC	Rescue co-ordination Center
RCDS	Raster Chart Display System
RCO	Regional Co-ordination Organization
RCPA	Range to Closest Point of Approach
RCS	Remote Control System
R.D	Relative Density
RDC	Running Down Clause (insurance)

RDF	Radio Direction Finder
RDF	Radio Direction Finder
RDM	Radiation Detection and Management
RDT	Radio Data Terminal
RDV	Rendezvous
REM	Rapid Eye Movement
REDES	Registered Excise Dealers & Shippers
REG	Regional (territory)
RES	Renewable Energy Source
RF	Radio frequency
RFDC	Radio Frequency data Communications
RFID	Radio Frequency Identification
RFQ	Request For Quotation
RGSS	Register General of Shipping and Seaman

RH	Relative Humidity (meteorology)
RICS	Royal Institute of Chartered Surveyors
RID	International Carriage of Dangerous Goods By Rail
RIPI	Reversed Inland Point Intermodal
RINA	The Royal Institution of Naval Architecture
RITL	Radio In The Loop(network)
RLG	Ring Laser Gyro
ROG	Receipt Of Goods
ROK	Republic Of Korea
ROM	Read Only Memory (computer)
RON	Research Octane Number
ROSPA	Royal Society for the Prevention of Accidents
ROV	Remotely Operated Vehicle

ROW	Right Of Way
RM	Raw Materials
RMA	Returned Merchandise Authorization
RMC	Regional Meteorological Centre
RMC	Royal Mail Ship
RML	Relative Movement Line
RMS	Root Mean Square
RMS	Royal Mail Ship
RN	Royal Navy
RNC	Raster Nautical Charts
RNR	Royal Navy Reserve
RNSS	Radio Navigation Satellite Service
ROC	Running Down Clause
ROM	Read Only Memory
RORO	Roll-On/Roll-Off

RP	Recommended Price
RR	Radio Regulations
RRG	Rescue and Recovery Group
RRSP	Recommended Retail Selling Price
RSC	Rescue Sub- Centre
RSGT	Red Sea Gateway Terminal
RSP	Retail Selling Price
RSPL	Recommended Spares Parts List
RSS	Root Sum Square
RSV	Revised Standard Version
RSVP	Respondez, s'ill Vous Plait
RNAS	Royal Naval Air Service
RO-Pax	Roll On-Roll Off Passenger Vessel
RORO	Roll on-Roll off Ship
RoT	Rate of Turn

ROV	Remotely Operated Vehicle
RPI	Retail Price Index
RPM	Revolution Per Minute
RS	Reflected Sun
RSV	Revised Standard Version
RT	Radio Telephone
RTBA	Rate To Be Agreed
RTCM	Radio Technical Commission for Maritime Service
RTI	Renewable Transport Item
RTP	Regional transport Plan
RTP	Returnable Transit Packaging
RTR	Road Traffic Regulations
RTS	Regional Transport Strategy
RWMAC	Radioactive Waste Management Advisory Committee

Rx	Receiver
RYX	Royal Yacht Squadron

S

S	Second; Speed; Sand; South; Starboard
SAC	Strategic Air Command
SADT	Self-Accelerating Decomposition Temperature
SAJ	Shipbuilder Association of Japan
SALM	Single Anchor Leg Mooring
SAN	Storage Area Network
SAN	Shipping Advice Note
SAP	Safety Assessment/ Assurance Principles
SAPS	Sulphate Ash Phosphorous & Sulphur (emission)
SAR	Search and Rescue

SARBE	Search & Rescue Beacon Equipment
SARP	Search and Rescue Processor
SARS	Severe Acute Respiratory Syndrome (disease)
SART	search and Rescue Radar Transponder
SAR	Search and Rescue
SARR	Search and Rescue Repeater
SARSAT	Search & Rescue Rader Transponder
SART	Search and Rescue
SALM	Single Anchor Leg Mooring
SAM	System Area Monitor
SAS	Scandinavian Airline System
SAT	Ship Apparent Time
SATCOM	Satellite Communications
SB	Simultaneous Broadcast

SBAC	Small Business Advisory Centre
S.B.E	Stand By Engine
SBM	Single Buoy Mooring
SBN	Standard Book Number
SBS	Special Boat Service
SBT	Segregated Ballast Tank
SBV	Sea Bed Vehicle
SbW	South By West
SCA	Spill Control Association
SCBA	Self Contained Breathing Apparatus
SCC	Storage Connecting Circuit
SCF	Satellite Control Facility
SCI	Seamen's Church Institute
SCMESS	Society of Consulting Marine Engineers & Shop Surveyors

SCO	Surface Contaminated Objects
SCP	Simplified Clearance Procedures
SCP	Supply Chain Planning
SCR	Selective Catalytic Reduction System
SCS	Suez Canal Surcharge
SCT	Sharja Container terminal
SD	Special Delivery
SD	Semi Diameter
SD	Sounding Doubtful
SDP	Search Data Provider
SDR	Special Drawings Rights (Int. Monitory Sys.)
SDS	Simplified Delivery System
SE	South East
SEDAR	Submerged Electrode Detection & Ranging

SEEMP	Ship Emergency Efficiency Management Plan
SEF	Shipbuilding Employers' Federation
SEM	Single European Market
SENC	System Electronic Navigation Chart
SES	Ship Earth Station
SE	Stock Exchange
SEATO	South Asia Treaty Organization
SENC	System Electronic Navigational charts
SEO	satellite for Earth Observation
SFFF	Salt Free Fat Free
SF	Secondary Face Factor
S.F	Stowage Factor
SFP	Structural Fire Protection
SG	Solicitor General

SG	Ship and Goods
SG	Specific Gravity
SH	Ship's Head (heading)
SHC	Super High Cube (container)
SHA	Sidereal Hour Angle
SHF	Super High Frequency
SHPD	Super High Performance Diesel
SI	International System of Units
SI	Statutory Instrument
SIB	Shipbuilding Industry Board
SICGE	Special Intermediate Common General Equipment
SID	Speed Indicator Device
SID	Sudden Ionosphere Disturbance
SIDS	Ship's Installation Drawings

SIDS	Small Island Developing State
SIGTTO	Society of International Gas Tanker & Terminal Operator
SIM	Subscriber Identity Module
SIN	Substance Identification Number
SINS	Ship's Internal Navigation System
SIRC	Seafarers International Research Centre
SIS	Satellite Information Service
SITPRO	Simplification of International Trade Procedures Board
SIUNA	Seafarers International Union of North America
SLD	Sea Level Datum
SL	Salvage Loss (insurance)
SL	Source Language

SL&C	Shippers' Load and Count
SLD	Self Locking Device
SLF	Sub-Committee on Stability & load Lines & on Fishing Vessels' Safety
SMC	Safety Management Certificate
SMCP	Standard Marine Communication Phrase
SMG	Speed Made Good
SMRTB	Ship & Marine Requirements Technology Board
SMS	Safety Management System
SMS	Security & Management Service
SMS	Ship Motion Simulator
SMS	Short Message System/ Service
SMS	Synchronous Meteorological Satellite
SMT	Ship Mean Time

SNG	Satellite News Gathering
SNG	Secured Network Gateway
SNG	Substitute Natural Gas
SNG	Synthetic Natural Gas
SNLR	Service No Longer Required
SNR	Single-to-Noise Ratio
SOA	Speed Of Advance
SOG	Speed Over Ground
SOHC	Single Overhead Cam (shaft)
SOI	Southern Oscillation Indicator
SOL	Ship Owner's Liability
SOLAS	Safety of Life At Sea
SOLE	Society Of Logistics Engineers
SONAR	Sound Navigation & Ranging
SOP	Standard Operating Procedures

SOPEP	Ships Oil Pollution Emergency Plan
SOS	Save Our Souls
SOTDMA	Self-Organizing Time Division Multiple Access
SPA	Special Protection Area
SPA	Sudden Phase Anomaly
SPC	Self Polishing Copolymer (anti Fouling Paint)
SPEC	South Pacific Bureau for Economic Co-operation
SPI	Service Performance Indicator
SPL	Sound Pressure Level
SPM	Single Point Mooring
SPOC	Single Point of Contact
SPR	Sulphate Resistant Cement
SPS	Special Purposes Ship

SPS	Standard Position Service
Sq	Sequel (meteorology)
SRM	Speed Of Relative Movement
SRNA	Shipbuilders & Repairs National Association
SRU	Search & Rescue Unit
SRV	Shuttle & Re-gasification vessel
SS	Signal Station
SS	Expanding Square Search
SS	Steam Ship
SSA	Ship Building & Ship Repair Association
SSAS	Ship Security Alert System
SSN	Standard Serial Number
SSN	Standard Shipping Note
SSR	Secondary Surveillance Rader

SSS	Short Sea Shipping
SSSI	Site of Special Scientific Interest
SSSS	Space Shuttle System Specification
SST	Super Sonic Transport
ST	Standard Time
ST	Shipping Ticket
STACO	Standing Committee for the Study of Principles of Standards
STC	Said To Contain
STC	scientific & Technical Committee
STC	Sensitivity Time Control
STCW	Standard of Training, Certification and Watch keeping
STO	sea Transport Officer
STP	Standard temperature and Pressure
STPR	Strategic Transport Projects Review

STRC	Scientific & Technological Research Committee
STW	Space Technology Centre
STW	Speed Through Water
SU	Search Unit
SURV	Standard Underwater research Vessel
SV	Surrender Value (insurance)
SW	Shipper's Weight
SW	Salt Water/ Sea water
SWAT	Special Weapon & Tactics
SWATH	Small Water plane Area Twin Hull
SWB	Sea Way Bill
SWG	Standard Wire Gauge
SWL	Safe Working Load
SWOT	Strengths, Weaknesses, Opportunities and Threats (risks).

SWP	Safe Working Pressure
SWPA	South West Pacific Area
SWR	Standing Wave Ratio
SWR	Steel Wire Rope
SX	Sundays Excepted
SYR	Syria
SZ	Size

T

T	Temperature
TACA	Transatlantic Conference Agreement
TACS	Total Access Communications System
TACV	Tracked Air-Cushion Vehicle`
TAI	International Automatic Time
Tal	Traffic and Accidents Loss

TAPLINE	Trans-Arabian Pipe-Line
TAZ	Traffic Analysis Zone
TB	True Bearing
TBD	To Be Decided
TBL	Through Bill of Loading (insurance)
TBS	Talks Between Ships
TBT	Tributylin
TC	True Course/ Time Charter
TCA	Time of Satellite Closest Approach
TCC	Technology Consultancy Centre
TCPA	Time of Closest Point of Approach
TCU	Terminal Control Unit
TD	Time Difference
TDDL	Time Division Data Link
TDMA	Time Division Multiple Access Network

TDO	Tornado (meteorology)
TDOP	Time Dilution Of Precession
TDRSS	Tracking and Data relay Satellite System
TDT	Terrestrial Dynamical Time
TEMPSC	Totally Enclosed Motor Propelled Survival Craft
TER	Transcutaneous Electrical Resistance
TER	Total Expense Ratio
TER	Total External Reflection
TER	Training Evaluation Report
TER	Telecommunication Electrical Room
TER	Total Engine Revolution
TESSA	Tax Exempt Special Saving Account
TEUS	Twenty-Foot Eequivalent Unit
TFS	Total Floor Space

TH	True Heading
THL	Terminal Handling Loading
TIC	Taking Into Consideration (low)
TIC	Total Inventory Cost (value)
TICS	Traffic Information & Control System
TIMCON	Timber Packing & Pallet Confederation
TKB	Tanker Barge
TLV	Threshold Limit Value
TMC	Transmitting Magnetic Compass
TMCP	Thermo-Mechanically Controlled Processed
TMG	Track Made Good
TML	Three Mile Limit
TNTC	Too Numerous TO Count
TOD	Time of Delivery/ Day

TOGA	Test Of General Ability
TOR	Telex Over Radio
TORCH	Transferring Ownership Responsibility & Commitment For Hazard Control
TOS	Total Order Shipped
TOT	Training of Trainer
TP	Third Party (insurance)
TPA	Thermal Protective Aid
TPC	Tones Per Centimeter
TPO	Third Party Only (insurance)
TPPD	Third Party Property Damage (insurance)
TPQ	Theoretical Pallet Quantity
TQC	Total Quality Control
TRC	Type Rating Certificate
TRL	Transport Research Laboratory

TRM	Trade Mark
TRS	Tropical Revolving Storm
TS	True Sun
TSC	Total Supply Cost (value)
TSS	Traffic Separation Scheme
TSS	Turbine Steam Ship
TT	Telegraphic Transfer
TT	Ticket Ticker
TT	Transit Time
TT&C	Tracking Telemetry and Command (satellite)
TTFF	Time To First Fix
TTG	Time To Go
TTSF	Time To Subsequent Fix
TU	Trade Union

TU	Transmission Unit
TUC	Trade Union Congress
TURB	Turbulence (meteorology)
TURN	Trader Unique Reference Number (custom)
TUS	Total Units Shipped (number)
Tw	Tare Weight
TWI	The Welding Institute
TWIC	Transportation Worker Identification Credential
TWIC	Transportation Worker Identity Card
TWIC	The World Internet
TWIMC	To Whom It May Concern
TWO	This Week Only
TWOC	Taken Without Owner Consent
TWS	Total Weight Shipped

TWU	Transport Workers Union (US)
Tx	Transmitter
TYPOE	Ten Year Plan for Ocean Exploration
TZn	True Zenith Distance

<u>U</u>

U	Upper Limb correction
UAE	United Arab Emirates
UARP	Universal Acoustic Range & Processor
UBS	Universal Bulk Ship
UCATT	Union of Construction, Allied Trades, & Technique
UCP	Uniform Customs & Practice for Documentary Credit
UCS	Uniform Container Symbol
UDC	Universal Decimal Classification

UDE	Undesirable Effect
UDL	Uniformly Distributed Load
UEL	Upper Explosion Limit
UERD	Underwater Explosions Research Division
UERE	User Equivalent Range Error
UFL	Upper Flammable Limit
UFO	Unidentified Flying Objects
UHF	Ultra High Frequency
UHP	Ultra High Pressure
UI	User Interface
UIN	Unit Identity Number
UK	United Kingdom
UKC	Under Keel Clearance
UKHIS	UK Hazard Information System

UKHO	United Kingdom Hydrographic Office
UKOOA	United Kingdom Offshore Operator Association
UKOPP	United Kingdom Oil Pollution Prevention (certificate)
UL	Upper Limb
ULA	Union of International Associations
ULBC	Ultra Large Bulk Carrier
ULCC	Ultra Large Crude Carrier
ULDR	Unit Load Device Rates (shipping)
ULSGO	Ultra Low Sulphur Gas Oil
UMS	Unmanned Machinery Space
UNCED	United Nation Conference on Environmental
UNCTAD	United Nations Conference on Trade and Development
UNDP	United Nations Development Program

UNDPKO	United Nations Department for Peacekeeping Operations
UNDRO	United Nations Disaster Relief Organization
UNECE	United Nations Economic Commission for Europe
UNEP	United Nations Environmental Program
UNEC	United Nations Economic Commission For Europe
UNEP	United Nations Environment Program
UNESCO	United Nations Educational, Scientific & Cultural Organization
UNFCOC	United Nations Convention On Climate Change
UNHCR	United Nations Higher Commission for Refugees
UNICEF	United Nations International Children's Emergency Fund

UNIDO	United Nations Industrial Development Organization
UNITA	United Nations Institute for Training & Research
UNO	United Nations Organization
UNRRA	United Nations Relief & Rehabilitation Administration
UNRISD	United Nations Research Institute for Social
UNS	United Nations System
UNTDI	United Nations Trade Data Interchange
UOM	Unit Of Measure
UPC	Uniform(Universal)Product Code
UPD	United Port District
UPR	Unearned Premium s Reserve (insurance)
UPS	Uninterruptible Power Supply

UPS	United Parcel Service
UPS	Universal Polar Stereographic
UPU	Universal Postal Union
UQ	Ultra Quick Flashing
URE	User Range Error
USA	United States of America
USB	Universal Serial Bus
USB	Upper Sideband of Radio Signal
USCG	United State Coast Guard
USD	United States Dollar
USFRA	US Freight Rate Average
USGS	United States Geodetic Survey
USL	Upper Specification Limit
USM	United State Mail
USMMA	US Merchant Marine Academy

USN	United State Navy
USNA	United State Naval Academy
USS	United State Service/Ship
USSB	United States Shipping Board
USSS	United States Steam Ship
UST	Ultra Stream Turbine
USWMS	United State Waterway Marking System
UT	Universal Time
UT	Unaccompanied Trailer
UTC	Coordinated Universal Time
UTC	Used Truck Center
UTM	Universal TransverseMercator
UV	Ultra Violet

V

V	Variation; Vertex
VAT	Value Added Tax
VAB	Voice Answer Back
VAD	Voluntary Aid Detachment
VAV	Variable Air Volume
VCE	Variable Cycle Engine
VCG	Vertical center of gravity
VCP	Video Cassette Player
VCR	Video Cassette Recorder
VD	Venereal Disease
VDOP	Vertical Dilution Of Precision
VDR	Voyage Data Recorder
VDT	Visual Display Terminal

VDU	Visual Display Unit
VES	Volunteer Emergency Service
VES	Voyage Efficiency System
VFD	Volunteer Fire Department
VF	Visual Field
VFI	Vertical Force Instrument
VFR	Visiting Friends and Relatives(passenger)
VG	Very Good
VHD	Very High Density
VHF	Very High Frequency
VHE	Very High Energy
VHSD	Very High Speed Data
VIN	Vehicle Identification Number
VIP	Very Important Person
VIPH	Very Important Person's Hall

VIS	Visibility (meteorology)
VLBC	Very Large Bulk Carrier
VLCC	Very Large Crude Carrier
VLCT	Very Large Commercial Transport
VLF	Vehicle License Fee
VLF	Very Low Frequency
VLGC	Very Large Gas Carrier
VLOC	Very Large Ore Carrier
VLR	Very Long Range
VLS	Vertical Launching System
VMG	Variable Message System
VMG	Velocity Made Good
VMS	Voice Message System
VMU	Vehicle Maintenance Unit
VNS	Vehicle Navigation System

VOC	Volatile Organic Compound
VOCA	Victims of Crime Act
VOHMA	The International Vessel Operation Hazardous Materials Association
VP	Vice President
VPF	Vector Product format
VPH	Vehicle Per Hour
VPN	Virtual Private Network
VR	Variable Route
VRM	Variable Range Marker
VSII	Very Seriously Ill or Injured
VT	Vacuum Tube
VT	Variable Time
VTMS	Vessel Traffic Management System
VTOL	Vertical Take-off & Landing

VTR	Video Tape Recorder
VTS	Vessel Traffic System/Tracking System/Service

#

W	West; White
WADGPS	Wide Area Differential Global Positioning System
WAN	Wide Area Network
WAP	Web Application Project
WALN	Wireless Automation Level Network
WAP	Wireless Access Point
WAP	Wireless Application Protocol
WAP	Waste Analysis Plan
WAP	Web Application Project
WAP	Wired Access Point

WAP	Wireless Access Protocol
WARC	World Administrative Radio Council
WAST	West Australia Standard Time
WAT	Wing Assisted Trim
WATS	Wide-Area Telecommunications Service
WB	Weather Bureau
WBT	Water Ballast Tank
WE	Watch Error
WB	Way Bill
WC	Water Closet
WC	Without Charge
WCI	Waterways Council, Incorporation
WCL	World Confederation of Labor
WCO	World Custom Organization
WCUK	West Cost of United Kingdom

WFP	World Food Program
WFTU	World Federation of Trade Union
WEARCON	Weather Observation & Forecasting Control System
WEC	World Energy Conference
WGC	World Gas Conference
WGS	World Geodetic System/Survey
WGT	World Gross Tonnage
WHMIS	Workplace Hazardous Materials Information System
WHO	World Health Organization
WHR	Waste Recovery System
WIF	Water In Fuel System
WIP	Work In Progress
WL	Water Line
WL	Wave Length

WL	Wide Load
WL	Waiting List
WLAN	Wireless Local Area Network
WLL	Wireless Local Loop(communications)
WLN	Weapon Logistic Network
WMD	weapon of Mass Destruction
WMO	World Meteorological Organization
WNA	Winter North Atlantic
WNL	Within Normal Limit
WNTI	World Nuclear Transport Institute
WO	Written Order
WOC	Without Compensation
WOF	Warranty Of Fitness
WOR	Without Responsibility
WOT	War On Terrorism

WPA	With Particular Average (insurance)
WP	Waypoint/ Weather Permitting
WP	Word Processor
WPB	Waste –Paper Basket
WPC	Wave Piercing Catamaran
WPC	World Product Code
WPC	World Customs Organization
WNA	Winter North Atlantic
WPC	Wave Piercing Catamaran
WPC	World Peace Council
WPM	Word per Minute
WR	War Risk (insurance)
WRC	World Radio Communication Conference
WR,SR&CC	War Risk, Strikes, Riots & Civil Commotion's

WRI	War Risk Insurance (insurance)
WRO	War Risk Only (insurance)
WSP	Water Supply Point
WT	Watch Time
W/T	Wireless Telegraphy
WTC	World Trade Centre
WTD	Water Tight Door
WTO	World Trade Organization
WTTG	Wales Timber Transport Group
WW	Warehouse Warrant
WWDSHEX	Weather Working Days, Sundays & Holidays Excluded
WWI	World War I
WWNWS	World Wide Navigational Warning Service
WWW	World Wide Web

WWW	World Weather Watch
WWX	World Wide Express
WX	Weather (meteorology)

X	Parallax Angle
XA	Mexico (country)
XC	Cross Country
XDOP	Cross-Track
XMTR	Transmitter
XTE	Cross Track Error

Y

Y	Yellow (color)
Y2K	Year 2000
YAR	Yemen (country)
YB	Year Book
YMBA	Yacht and Motorboat Association
YOB	Year Of Birth
YTD	Year To Date

Z

Z	Azimuth
ZAC	Zone Access Control
ZD	Zenith Distance
ZD	Zone Description

ZIP	Zone Improvement Plan
ZR	Freezing Rain (meteorology)
ZST	Zone Standard Time
ZT	Zone Time
ZIP	Zone Improvement Plan
ZL	Zero Line
ZOPA	Zone of Possible Agreement
ZPG	Zero Population Growth
ZT	Zone Time

المصادر

01-GMDSS	IMO
02-MARPOL	IMO
03-IPP	IMO
03-SOLAS	IMO
04-OCEAN PASSAGE FOR THE WOLRD UK HYDROGAPHIC	
05-ADMIRALITY SAILING DIRECTION UK HYDROGRAPHIC OFFICE	
06-ADMIRALITY LIST OF RADIO SIGNALS	IMO
07-ADMIRALITY LIST OF LIGHTS AND FOG SIGNALS IMO	
08-IMDG CODE	IMO
09-INTERNATIONAL CODE OF SIGNALS IMO	
10-RADAR OBSERVER HAND BOOK W.BURGER	

11-RADAR & ARPA MANUAL	ALAN BOLE
12-SHIP STABILITY	DERRITT
13-SEAMANSHIP TECHNIQUE	D J HOUSE
14-TANKER HANDBOOK FOR DECK OFFICER BAPTIST	
15-LIFE SAVING APPLIANCES	IMO
16-MASTER'S BUSINESS COMPANION MALCOLM	
17-SHIP REGISTRATION LAW & PRACTICE CHARD COLES	
18-THE INSTITUTE TIME CLAUSES HULL, ROBERT BROWN	
19-Guide to Port Entry UK Hydrographic	
20Mariner's Hand book UK Hydrographic	

21-Tidal Stream Atlas
UK Hydrographic
22-Notices to Mariners
UK Hydrographic
23-Sailing Directions and pilot book
UK Hydrographic
24-Other different sources

INDEX

01	A	7-25
02	B	25-29
03	C	30-47
04	D	47-56
05	E	56-65
06	F	65-76
07	G	77-84
08	H	84-87
09	I	88-104
10	J	104-105
11	K	106-107
12	L	107-118
13	M	118-127

14	N	128-136
15	O	137-142
16	P	142-152
17	Q	152-153
18	R	153-160
19	S	160-173
20	T	173-180
21	U	180-186
22	V	187-191
23	W	191-197
24	X	197-198
25	Y	198
26	z	198-199
المصادر	--	201
INDEX	--	205

Printed in the United States
By Bookmasters